Basic Budgeting
You Can Do It!

By

Bill Byrd

3rd Edition

Basic Budgeting: You Can Do It!

1. Budgeting 2.Personal Finance 3. Saving Money
ISBN 978-0-557-40126-0

Bill Byrd
Email: BillVickiByrd@att.net

I want to thank the following people who reviewed and helped improve the content of this booklet.

My wife Vicki,
Our family,
Rev. D Scott Johnson,
Rev. Joe Mitchell,
Gina and Jason O'Brien,
Bill O'Patterson,
Rev. Todd Outcalt,
Rev. Jerry Rairdon,
Steve & Marla Ramsey,
Jeremiah Stump

4

The Big Question

Where does all the money go?

Week after week we spend the majority of our lives working. We get paid. We pay the bills. Here and there we go out to eat and take in a movie. When we make a major purchase or go on vacation, we usually have to borrow the money or charge it.

When we stop to evaluate how things are going, sometimes we ask, "Where does all the money go?" Our savings never grows. The bills never seem to go away! Where does it all go?

Month after month, year after year, thousands of dollars just seem to slip right through our fingers and we end up with nothing to show for it! Too often we really do not know where the money goes because we just do not have a way to keep track of how we spend or save what we make.

This booklet was created to help you solve that problem.

You can read this booklet from cover to cover in about an hour. Then you will be ready to put together your budgeting plan. At that point you will have a simple, easy to understand budget which will help you plan and control your spending.

Use it as a guide every payday and I think you will find that you will get a lot more out of life. You will have less stress about your personal finances. You will waste less money. You will save more money, and you will be able to do more with what you have!

My Situation

Early on I had the privilege of being poor! Yes, you read that right!

Here's a true story.

One time when I was a kid our family took a vacation. Beforehand my dad said to my mom, "We have $98!" He handed her $49. "When my half is gone we're turning around!" he finished.

We were going to Florida on **_ninety-eight_** bucks! I was pumped!

We packed the Coleman stove, canned meat (Spam), a bag of potatoes and a thermos filled with Kool-Aid in the trunk with our clothes. The rear of the car was nearly dragging the ground. We left home about four in the morning. I was half asleep. But hey, we were going to Florida!

On the road it didn't take long for me to find out that, no matter how many times I asked, on $98 we wouldn't be stopping at Stuckey's or Joe's Alligator farm or any other place with an admission fee or a gift shop. It was a "no budget" vacation.

We sure didn't stay at any nice motels. In fact, for most of the trip mom and dad slept on the picnic tables at roadside parks while we three kids slept on the seats in the car. Amazingly, in spite of our lack of money we made it all the way around the tip of southern Florida. I can still remember driving through the hot sweaty Florida Everglades across what they called the Tamiami Trail. Every so often we could see a Seminole Indian family living on a platform a couple feet off the ground with nothing but a thatched roof for shelter. Now they really were poor! They couldn't even afford a $98 vacation!

I married my wife Vicki when I was a brash twenty–three year old. She was twenty-one. We were two young pups who had no idea how to handle our money. Our big financial plan was "Make it and spend it all!" And we did!

It sure didn't take long for that plan to create issues. Just one week after getting married we were in an auto accident. A lady in a big Oldsmobile rammed us in the rear end and totaled our car. Our solution? We immediately bought a brand new Mustang **_on credit of course_**.

Well, as you can imagine, after making a few decisions like that our finances got to be pretty tight. Our bills quickly exceeded our income. Over time we had our first child and then a second. As our family grew that Mustang just didn't work for our family anymore. I remember the back seat being filled with our kids and our groceries which were squashed onto the floor behind the front seats. The final blow came when we bought an artificial Christmas tree which we couldn't get into the car to take it home. It was time for a vehicle upgrade.

So we bought a Station Wagon, again on credit. Soon after that we had our third child. Then a bit later the car broke down. The water heater started leaking. My wife Vicki had heart surgery. We had no savings. We had income but we had no money! Simply put, we were poor! We were spending more than we made!

Not long after that a couple we knew complained that their savings had just dropped below a hundred dollars. Vicki and I looked at each other and laughed. We could not remember a single time when our savings had been ***above*** a hundred dollars!

After ten years of marriage I followed a call from God to go into ministry. We sold our home, I quit my job and with three small children we moved to Delaware Ohio where I would attend seminary. When we landed there in our two bedroom apartment with our three children, for the first time in our life we qualified for ***Welfare***. Wow, was that humbling!

Even though we both had jobs we had no choice. We took the help from the government.

It was then that the life lessons really began. Day after day we had to find a way to get the most out of every dollar we made. We certainly did not have money to waste. We had a big challenge.

So we began to use a budget to keep an eye on our spending.

Beginning to budget both our income and expenditures put us on the road toward a happier life.

After years of foolish uncontrolled spending we finally learned the value of creating and ***using*** a simple budget. That one act alone helped us survive a period of time when we had nothing much but debt.

Again and again our simple approach to budgeting has helped us during a number of other "we are nearly broke" periods. As a result of what we learned during those periods of poverty we are now able to use and save our money much more wisely.

Others Have the Same Problem!

Over the years I have noticed that other people have the same problem. Over and over I have heard people talk about their struggles to keep track of their finances. I have heard people say stuff like: "Payday is a real headache!" or "Why can't we afford to take a vacation?" or "We seem to argue a lot about money!"

On a number of those occasions I have had the chance to share how my wife and I have used a simple budget to overcome some of the very same problems. Without discussing the details of their personal situations, I have shared the budgeting approach we have used for years.

In each and every one of those situations I received a big "*Thank You*!" from the person for helping them discover a way to get a handle on their personal finances. One young man even emailed me months after one of those sharing sessions to thank me for telling him about our budgeting ideas. The impact of budgeting on his life and marriage was transforming.

Basic Budgeting

Now there are hundreds of ways to put together a budget. Just ask a few of your friends or visit the Personal Finance section of the local bookstore or library. You will see that I am right.

Some of those budgeting systems are pretty complicated beasts. Most books on budgeting have hundreds of pages. Just the other day I saw one which had **_over 1100 pages_**! You've got to be kidding me! None of the books that I saw that day would ever be described as simple.

Personally, I always vote for simplicity. The simple budgeting approach I've shared with the folks I mentioned above **_is included in full in this booklet_**. I intentionally made this booklet brief and to the point.

In one evening, using this approach, you **_can_** put together a budget (a spending and savings plan) that is easy to understand and use.

With this approach you can create your budget with a pencil, paper and a calculator. Of course you may also choose to set up your budget using a computer tool like Microsoft Excel. Email me and I will send you an Excel Basic Budgeting template. (BillVickiByrd@att.net)

The main thing is that this simple approach to budgeting will quickly help you get a handle on how you spend what you make and help you save some of it along the way.

When you have your budget put together I think you will discover that (1) knowing where your money is going and (2) having a way to plan financially for the future makes a huge difference in your life.

In fact, I would venture to say that **_your life will be happier_**!

That in itself makes putting a budget together worthwhile.

Ok. Turn the page and let's take a look at how you can build a simple budget.

A Sample Budget

In the next few pages we will build a **one month** budget for a fictitious Bill & Vicki!
(Of course you should know that all the numbers are made up)

The first section of the budget records how much money our pretend Bill & Vicki have to pay their bills. Give it a look.

Bill & Vicki's Budget	Pay Date		Pay Date	
	Jan 15th	Notes	Jan 31st	Notes
Money available to pay bills				
Bill's take home pay	850.00		850.00	
Vicki's take home pay	850.00		850.00	
Checking account				
Cash				
Other Money				
Total available to pay bills	1700.00		1700.00	

Figure 1

Notice:

- Bill and Vicki are both paid twice a month. On the 15th and at the end of the month. (Your payday may be every week or every other week. Use the interval which is correct for your situation)
- Each payday they will insert the amount they have left over in their checking account.
- They also will insert the amount of cash they have available.
- The "Other Money" line leaves room to include money they may receive from time to time from gifts, yard sales, tax returns, etc.
- The total line indicates how much money they have to pay their bills each payday.

Pretty simple!

Ok, let's check out the next section of their budget.

Bills to be paid with a check or on-line payment

Bills to be paid by check or EFT	Jan 15th	Notes	Jan 31st	Notes
Place of worship	135.00		135.00	
Apartment Rent - Due on the 1st			850.00	
Car payment - Due on the 20th	355.00			
Auto insurance - Due on the 10th			145.00	
License plates - both cars - Due in March				
Cell phones - Due on the 18th	85.00			
Cable TV - Due on the 25th	135.00			
Water - Due on the 10th			40.00	
Gas - Due on the 28th	95.00			
Electricity - Due on the 10th			60.00	
Visa - Due on the 15th	110.00			
Miscellaneous			75.00	Dentist
Total paid with checks or EFT	915.00		1305.00	

Figure 2

Notice:

- Each estimated or actual bill amount is entered under the appropriate pay date just *before* the bill's due date.

  Example: The car payment is due on the 20th of each month. So we include it to be paid on the 15th.

  Example: The Auto Insurance, Water and Electricity bills are due on the 10th of each month. So Bill & Vicki will plan to pay those February bills the payday before at the end of January.

  TIP - Pay your bills before the due date and avoid paying late fees and save some money!!

  TIP – Here's a really important tip! Pay a few extra dollars each month on your mortgage or car payment and you will pay thousands less in interest and pay off the loan much more quickly.

- Some of their bills are not paid every month. For example the Dentist bill is only paid once at the end of January.

- We've included a line for License Plate fees which will be paid in March.

- The total line indicates how much they will pay each payday with checks or on-line EFT.

Bills to be Paid with Cash

Some folks might say you don't need this "paid with cash" section. After all don't most people pay for almost everything with a Credit or Debit card? Sure they do! It is also true that ***most people are spending more than they make***. Simply put, I think Credit and Debit cards make it way too easy for me to spend my hard earned money!

Nothing slows down our spending more than having to pull those green backs out of our pocket and then hand them over to someone else. Start paying for your purchases with cash and you will start asking, "Do I really want to spend this money!"

Here is the cash part of Bill & Vicki's budget.

Items to be paid with Cash:	Jan 15th	Notes	Jan 31st	Notes
Groceries	140.00		140.00	
Bill's Auto Gas	80.00		80.00	
Vicki's Auto Gas	50.00		50.00	
Allowances (Vicki 40, Bill 40)	80.00		80.00	
Housing Allowance	35.00		35.00	
Entertainment	60.00		60.00	
Miscellaneous				
Total paid with cash	445.00		445.00	

Figure 3

Notice:
- To avoid confusion the cash for each item will be set aside in a marked envelope, a container, or in a special place in Vicki's purse or Bill's billfold.
- Each payday a limited amount of cash is set aside for groceries and gas. Bill and Vicki will only exceed the budgeted amount when necessary and then they have agreed that additional money must come from savings or other cash. ***Nothing*** will be charged on Credit or Debit cards.
- Both Bill & Vicki get a $40 cash allowance. Either of them can save/give/spend their allowance anyway they want without discussion. ***This item alone will save a lot of arguments***!
- The Housing Allowance will allow Bill & Vicki to buy the incidental items they need around the house. (Waste baskets, throw rugs, plants for the yard etc.)
- Entertainment cash will allow them to enjoy a movie or dinner without raiding another fund. However when the entertainment money is gone they must agree that it is time for them to stay home and watch TV or get a free movie from the local library.
- The total line indicates how much they pay with cash each payday.

Savings to be set aside

Savings to be set aside	Jan 15th	Notes	Jan 31st	Notes
Savings - Emergency fund	25.00		25.00	
Savings - Vacation	50.00		50.00	
Savings - Christmas gifts				
Savings - Retirement	50.00		50.00	
Other				
Total savings to be set aside	125.00		125.00	

Figure 4

Savings is the last, but maybe the most important, section of the budget.

This section allows Bill & Vicki to plan the amount they want to save each payday. At the end of each bill paying session they will transfer (EFT) the total savings amount into their *savings* account. Setting money aside in a "*savings only*" account will discourage them from spending it on other expenses.

Notice:

- Emergency Fund - Every payday Bill and Vicki will transfer money into their savings account for their emergency fund.

    o This money will ***not*** be left in the checking account.
    o It will ***not*** be placed in an envelope around the house.
    o It will only be withdrawn from savings in the event of an emergency.

You may ask "When should emergency funds be used?" or "What constitutes an emergency?"

We consider an emergency as any expense which ***must*** be paid that was ***not in the budget***. Here are some examples.

Emergencies

    o Insurance deductible to be paid after an auto accident.
    o Hospital bills received after unexpected gall bladder surgery.
    o Replacing a failing home furnace.

Not an Emergency

    o Buying a new car.
    o Taking a vacation.
    o Buying Christmas presents for the family.

- Vacation savings – It is amazing how much more fun you can have on vacation when you know it is already paid for. And you'll probably have more than $98 to spend! Having the cash up front also helps reduce the vacation cost because you won't end up paying vacation expenses with a credit card and then end up paying interest for months on what you charged.

- Christmas gifts – Budgeting dollars ahead of time for gifts will reduce the stress of holiday shopping. Because they have set money aside beforehand Bill & Vicki can buy the presents they want to purchase when they see them on sale well before the holiday rush (We start setting aside cash for Christmas in September). Less stress and save money! How's that for a plus!

- Retirement – It used to be that our employers provided a pension when we retire. That monthly income along with Social Security set people up pretty good when they retired. Those days are disappearing if not gone. Some projections indicate the Social Security system will be soon be in trouble too. So your personal savings will be a huge key to your retirement planning.

  The time for you to begin saving for retirement is _**now**_! Put aside those dollars in a secure fund and make them _**untouchable**_. Before you know it you will be ready to retire. Saving a little every payday, starting now, will help assure that you will have the money you need to retire when the times comes.

- Periodic bills (Escrow) – Annual homeowner's insurance, once a year school expenses, college tuition, quarterly road service, next car savings etc. should go in the savings section too.

  How much do I need to save ahead of time? Here are a couple examples.

  School Expenses

  Many families have "start of school" expenses every year in August. Say you want to have $400 to spend on clothes and school supplies for each of your three children. If you don't plan for it that $1200 expense every August can really mess up your finances.

  But if in September you begin saving $50 every payday for school expenses when August arrives next year you will have $1200 in savings to pay for those clothes, books etc. No charge card will be needed. No interest to pay. No scrimping on other expenses.

  Vacation

  Let's say you want to take a special vacation two years from now to celebrate that special anniversary. You estimate that the travel, hotels, food, admissions and spending money total $3,600.

  Begin saving now. Put aside just $75 each payday and when vacation time arrives in two years you will get on the plane knowing that everything is paid ($150 x 24 months = $3600). That will make it a much happier trip.

Save ahead and when the bill comes due transfer the money from savings and you will have the cash to pay for it without pain. If you begin planning ahead for these kinds of expenses you will eliminate a lot of stress from your life. So think ahead and put those items in your budget.

Well that's it. You've seen a sample of each section of the **Basic Budget**.

Now let's look at the entire one month budget…

ONE MONTH BUDGET

Bill & Vicki's Budget	Pay Date		Pay Date	
	Jan 15th	Notes	Jan 31st	Notes
Money available to pay bills				
Bill's take home pay	850.00		850.00	
Vicki's take home pay	850.00		850.00	
Checking account				
Cash				
Other Money				
Total available to pay bills	1700.00		1700.00	
Bills to be paid by check or EFT				
Place of worship	135.00		135.00	
Apartment Rent - Due on the 1st			850.00	
Car payment - Due on the 20th	355.00			
Auto insurance - Due on the 10th			145.00	
License plates - both cars - Due in March				
Cell phones - Due on the 18th	85.00			
Cable TV - Due on the 25th	135.00			
Water - Due on the 10th			40.00	
Gas - Due on the 28th	95.00			
Electricity - Due on the 10th			60.00	
Visa - Due on the 15th	110.00			
Miscellaneous			75.00	Dentist
Total paid with checks or EFT	915.00		1305.00	
Items to be paid with Cash:				
Groceries	140.00		140.00	
Bill's Auto Gas	80.00		80.00	
Vicki's Auto Gas	50.00		50.00	
Allowances (Vicki 40, Bill 40)	80.00		80.00	
Housing Allowance	35.00		35.00	
Entertainment	60.00		60.00	
Miscellaneous				
Total paid with cash	445.00		445.00	
Savings to be set aside				
Savings - Emergency fund	25.00		25.00	
Savings - Vacation	50.00		50.00	
Savings - Christmas gifts				
Savings - Retirement	50.00		50.00	
Other				
Total savings to be set aside	125.00		125.00	
Money Left Over/Short	215.00		(175.00)	

Figure 5

Notice:

1. One last line has been added. The "Money Left Over/Short" line tells Bill & Vicki if they will have enough money to pay the bills each payday. The goal is to have money left when the bills are paid.

   But what do you do with the left over money?

   Remember that many of your budget figures will be estimates. For example, unless you are on a budget plan your utility bills will vary each month.

   We leave up to $200 of our "money left over" in the checking account until the next bill paying cycle. This gives us a little reserve cash should the next payday's bills be a little more than we expect.

   However, if we happen to have a payday with a lot of "Money Left Over" we usually put the extra money in our savings account. But sometimes we will use some of it for a special treat like a movie and a meal, etc.

2. Negative or short amounts are enclosed in parentheses. ($175.00)

BILL & VICKI'S THREE MONTH BUDGET

Here we have added two additional months to the budget.

Bill & Vicki's Budget	Pay Date 1/15/2010	Notes	Pay Date 1/31/2010	Notes	Pay Date 2/15/2010	Notes	Pay Date 2/28/2010	Notes	Pay Date 3/15/2010	Notes	Pay Date 3/31/2010	Notes
Money available to pay bills												
Bill's take home pay	850.00		850.00		850.00		850.00		850.00		850.00	
Vicki's take home pay	850.00		850.00		850.00		850.00		850.00		850.00	
Checking account												
Cash												
Other Money							400.00	Tax Refund				
Total available to pay bills	1700.00		1700.00		1700.00		2100.00		1700.00		1700.00	
Bills to be paid by check or EFT												
Place of worship	135.00		135.00		135.00		180.00		135.00		135.00	
Apartment Rent - Due on the 1st			850.00				850.00				850.00	
Car payment - Due on the 20th	355.00				355.00				355.00			
Auto insurance - Due on the 10th			145.00				145.00				145.00	
License plates - both cars - Due in March							425.00					
Cell phones - Due on the 18th	85.00				85.00				85.00			
Cable TV - Due on the 25th	135.00				135.00				135.00			
Water - Due on the 10th			40.00				40.00				40.00	
Gas - Due on the 28th	95.00				95.00				95.00			
Electricity - Due on the 10th			60.00				60.00				60.00	
Visa - Due on the 15th	110.00				110.00				110.00			
Miscellaneous			75.00	Dentist								
Total paid with checks or EFT	915.00		1305.00		915.00		1700.00		915.00		1230.00	
Items to be paid with Cash:												
Groceries	140.00		140.00		140.00		140.00		140.00		140.00	
Bill's Auto Gas	80.00		80.00		80.00		80.00		80.00		80.00	
Vicki's Auto Gas	50.00		50.00		50.00		50.00		50.00		50.00	
Allowances (Vicki 40, Bill 40)	80.00		80.00		80.00		80.00		80.00		80.00	
Housing Allowance	35.00		35.00		35.00		35.00		35.00		35.00	
Entertainment	60.00		60.00		60.00		60.00		60.00		60.00	
Miscellaneous												
Total paid with cash	445.00		445.00		445.00		445.00		445.00		445.00	
Savings to be set aside												
Savings - Emergency fund	25.00		25.00		25.00		25.00		25.00		25.00	
Savings - Vacation	50.00		50.00		50.00		50.00		50.00		50.00	
Savings - Christmas gifts												
Savings - Retirement	50.00		50.00		50.00		50.00		50.00		50.00	
Other												
Total savings to be set aside	125.00		125.00		125.00		125.00		125.00		125.00	
Money Left Over/Short	215.00		(175.00)		215.00		(170.00)		215.00		(100.00)	

Figure 6

Notice we have included in the "Money available to pay bills" section an estimated amount for Bill & Vicki's tax refund in February.

Well that's it! We only need ***one page*** for their entire three month budget!

Wouldn't you agree? It is simple to create and easy to understand!

Everything looks pretty good except as we look at their budget we see a couple issues that need attention.

A Couple Issues

Bill & Vicki's Budget	Jan 15th	Notes	Jan 31st	Notes	Feb 15th	Notes	Feb 28th	Notes	Mar 15th	Notes	Mar 31st	Notes
Money available to pay bills												
Bill's take home pay	850.00		850.00		850.00		850.00		850.00		850.00	
Vicki's take home pay	850.00		850.00		850.00		850.00		850.00		850.00	
Checking account												
Cash												
Other Money							400.00	Tax Refund				
Total available to pay bills	1700.00		1700.00		1700.00		2100.00		1700.00		1700.00	
Bills to be paid by check or EFT												
Place of worship	135.00		135.00		135.00		180.00		135.00		135.00	
Apartment Rent - Due on the 1st			850.00				850.00				850.00	
Car payment - Due on the 20th	355.00				355.00				355.00			
Auto insurance - Due on the 10th			145.00				145.00				145.00	
License plates - both cars - Due in March							425.00					
Cell phones - Due on the 18th	85.00				85.00				85.00			
Cable TV - Due on the 25th	135.00				135.00				135.00			
Water - Due on the 10th			40.00				40.00				40.00	
Gas - Due on the 28th	95.00				95.00				95.00			
Electricity - Due on the 10th			60.00				60.00				60.00	
Visa - Due on the 15th	110.00				110.00				110.00			
Miscellaneous			75.00	Dentist								
Total paid with checks or EFT	915.00		1305.00		915.00		1700.00		915.00		1230.00	
Items to be paid with Cash:												
Groceries	140.00		140.00		140.00		140.00		140.00		140.00	
Bill's Auto Gas	80.00		80.00		80.00		80.00		80.00		80.00	
Vicki's Auto Gas	50.00		50.00		50.00		50.00		50.00		50.00	
Allowances (Vicki 40, Bill 40)	80.00		80.00		80.00		80.00		80.00		80.00	
Housing Allowance	35.00		35.00		35.00		35.00		35.00		35.00	
Entertainment	60.00		60.00		60.00		60.00		60.00		60.00	
Miscellaneous												
Total paid with cash	445.00		445.00		445.00		445.00		445.00		445.00	
Savings to be set aside												
Savings - Emergency fund	25.00		25.00		25.00		25.00		25.00		25.00	
Savings - Vacation	50.00		50.00		50.00		50.00		50.00		50.00	
Savings - Christmas gifts												
Savings - Retirement	50.00		50.00		50.00		50.00		50.00		50.00	
Other												
Total savings to be set aside	125.00		125.00		125.00		125.00		125.00		125.00	
Money Left Over/Short	215.00		(175.00)		215.00		(170.00)		215.00		(100.00)	

These pay periods are short!

Figure 7

On three different pay periods Bill & Vicki will not have enough money available to pay the bills. Notice the money left over figure is negative. Without a change those paydays will be very stressful!

Having a budget helps you see issues like this ahead of time. In this case Bill & Vicki can see "short" pay periods **_BEFORE_** they arrive!

There are a number of ways Bill & Vicki can plan for these "short" pay periods. Let's see what they might do.

BALANCING THE BUDGET

Bill & Vicki's Budget	Pay Date Jan 15th	Notes	Pay Date Jan 31st	Notes	Pay Date Feb 15th	Notes	Pay Date Feb 28th	Notes	Pay Date Mar 15th	Notes	Pay Date Mar 31st	Notes
Money available to pay bills												
Bill's take home pay	850.00		850.00		850.00		850.00		850.00		850.00	
Vicki's take home pay	850.00		850.00		850.00		850.00		850.00		850.00	
Checking account												
Cash												
Other Money							400.00	Tax Refund				
Total available to pay bills	1700.00		1700.00		1700.00		2100.00		1700.00		1700.00	
Bills to be paid by check or EFT												
Place of worship	135.00		135.00		135.00		180.00		135.00		135.00	
Apartment Rent - Due on the 1st			850.00				850.00				850.00	
Car payment - Due on the 20th	355.00				355.00				355.00			
Auto insurance - Due on the 10th	145.00				145.00						145.00	
License plates - both cars - Due in March							425.00					
Cell phones - Due on the 18th	85.00				85.00				85.00			
Cable TV - Due on the 25th	135.00				135.00				135.00			
Water - Due on the 10th	40.00				40.00						40.00	
Gas - Due on the 28th	95.00				95.00				95.00			
Electricity - Due on the 10th			60.00				60.00				60.00	
Visa - Due on the 15th	110.00				110.00				110.00			
Miscellaneous			75.00	Dentist								
Total paid with checks or EFT	1100.00		1120.00		1100.00		1515.00		915.00		1230.00	
Items to be paid with Cash:												
Groceries	140.00		140.00		140.00		140.00		140.00		110.00	
Bill's Auto Gas	80.00		80.00		80.00		80.00		80.00		80.00	
Vicki's Auto Gas	50.00		50.00		50.00		50.00		50.00		50.00	
Allowances (Vicki 40, Bill 40)	80.00		80.00		80.00		80.00		80.00		80.00	
Housing Allowance	35.00		35.00		35.00		35.00		35.00		0.00	
Entertainment	60.00		60.00		60.00		60.00		60.00		45.00	
Miscellaneous												
Total paid with cash	445.00		445.00		445.00		445.00		445.00		365.00	
Savings to be set aside												
Savings - Emergency fund	25.00		25.00		25.00		25.00		25.00		25.00	
Savings - Vacation	50.00		50.00		50.00		50.00		50.00		0.00	
Savings - Christmas gifts												
Savings - Retirement	50.00		50.00		50.00		50.00		50.00		50.00	
Other												
Total savings to be set aside	125.00		125.00		125.00		125.00		125.00		75.00	
Money Left Over/Short	30.00		10.00		30.00		15.00		215.00		30.00	

Note (Feb 28th / Mar 15th): Move the bill to the previous pay period.

Note (Mar 31st, cash items): Spend less on Groceries, Housing Allowance and Entertainment this pay period.

Note (Mar 31st, savings): No Vacation savings this pay period.

Figure 8

Bill and Vicki could employ two different budgeting strategies to balance their budget.

1) First, in January and February they could move the Auto Insurance and the Water Bill payments to an earlier payday when extra cash will be available. This would allow them to avoid charging the payment or paying the bill late and incurring late fees. This is a budgeting plus – saving money by avoiding credit card interest and late fees.

2) The second strategy they could use is to agree to spend less on groceries, housing allowance and entertainment at the end of March and to suspend their normal vacation savings deposit for that pay period only.

3) Of course a third option would be to get a part-time job or work overtime to make up the short fall. In this example that probably is not necessary.

As you can see having a **Basic Budget** allows you to see issues *before* they arise so you can make adjustments to avoid the problem entirely. Less arguments and a happier life! I like it!

A Balanced Budget

Bill & Vicki's Budget	Pay Date Jan 15th	Notes	Pay Date Jan 31st	Notes	Pay Date Feb 15th	Notes	Pay Date Feb 28th	Notes	Pay Date Mar 15th	Notes	Pay Date Mar 31st	Notes
Checking Account												
Bill's take home pay	850.00		850.00		850.00		850.00		850.00		850.00	
Vicki's take home pay	850.00		850.00		850.00		850.00		850.00		850.00	
Checking account												
Cash												
Other Money							400.00	Tax Refund				
Total available to pay bills	1700.00		1700.00		1700.00		2100.00		1700.00		1700.00	
Bills to be paid by check or EFT												
Place of worship	135.00		135.00		135.00		180.00		135.00		135.00	
Apartment Rent - Due on the 1st			850.00				850.00				850.00	
Car payment - Due on the 20th	355.00				355.00				355.00			
Auto insurance - Due on the 10th	145.00				145.00						145.00	
License plates - both cars - Due in March							425.00					
Cell phones - Due on the 18th	85.00				85.00				85.00			
Cable TV - Due on the 25th	135.00				135.00				135.00			
Water - Due on the 10th	40.00				40.00						40.00	
Gas - Due on the 28th	95.00				95.00				95.00			
Electricity - Due on the 10th			60.00				60.00				60.00	
Visa - Due on the 15th	110.00				110.00				110.00			
Miscellaneous			75.00	Dentist								
Total paid with checks or EFT	1100.00		1120.00		1100.00		1515.00		915.00		1230.00	
Items to be paid with Cash:												
Groceries	140.00		140.00		140.00		140.00		140.00		110.00	
Bill's Auto Gas	80.00		80.00		80.00		80.00		80.00		80.00	
Vicki's Auto Gas	50.00		50.00		50.00		50.00		50.00		50.00	
Allowances (Vicki 40, Bill 40)	80.00		80.00		80.00		80.00		80.00		80.00	
Housing Allowance	35.00		35.00		35.00		35.00		35.00		0.00	
Entertainment	60.00		60.00		60.00		60.00		60.00		45.00	
Miscellaneous												
Total paid with cash	445.00		445.00		445.00		445.00		445.00		365.00	
Savings to be set aside												
Savings - Emergency fund	25.00		25.00		25.00		25.00		25.00		25.00	
Savings - Vacation	50.00		50.00		50.00		50.00		50.00		0.00	
Savings - Christmas gifts												
Savings - Retirement	50.00		50.00		50.00		50.00		50.00		50.00	
Other												
Total savings to be set aside	125.00		125.00		125.00		125.00		125.00		75.00	
Money Left Over/Short	30.00		10.00		30.00		15.00		215.00		30.00	

Figure 9

Notice that by applying the above budget planning strategies Bill & Vicki will have a budget which has a positive "Money Left Over" line across the entire budgeting period.

At that point we can say their budget is **balanced**.

Some Observations

Now that their budget is put together and balanced Bill & Vicki can see where their money is going.

Each payday they can pull out their **Basic Budget**, make any adjustment necessary, and use it to guide their bill paying and saving. As they go along they can adjust their spending when needed.

They can relax knowing that they will be able to pay all their upcoming bills without encountering a shortage. They can rest easy knowing that they are adding to their savings and their emergency fund each payday.

Finally, each of them can spend their allowance money any way they want knowing that they will not impact their ability to pay their budgeted bills. That eliminates a lot of arguments and guilty feelings.

All in all life is good!

Until life happens!!! – Let's say that unexpectedly an auto accident occurs!

No one was hurt but Bill's car was totaled. The insurance company has written a check for the totaled vehicle. Bill has found two cars that he likes as replacements.

Car 1 - A recent model red convertible - Price $18,000. After making a down payment the monthly payment for that vehicle will be $550 per month. Insurance would be an additional $75.

Car 2 - A nice little pickup truck - Price $8,900. After making a down payment the monthly payment will be $300. Insurance would stay about the same.

Bill wants to discuss it with Vicki. She wisely suggests they look at the budget impact each vehicle would have.

YOUR BUDGET – A DECISION MAKING TOOL

Bill & Vicki's Budget	Pay Date Jan 15th	Notes	Pay Date Jan 31st	Notes	Pay Date Feb 15th	Notes	Pay Date Feb 28th	Notes	Pay Date Mar 15th	Notes	Pay Date Mar 31st	Notes
Checking Account												
Bill's take home pay	850.00		850.00		850.00		850.00		850.00		850.00	
Vicki's take home pay	850.00		850.00		850.00		850.00		850.00		850.00	
Checking account												
Cash												
Other Money							400.00	Tax Refund				
Total available to pay bills	1700.00		1700.00		1700.00		2100.00		1700.00		1700.00	
Bills to be paid by check or EFT												
Place of worship	135.00		135.00		135.00		180.00		135.00		135.00	
Apartment Rent - Due on the 1st			850.00				850.00				850.00	
Bill's Convertible	550.00				550.00				550.00			
Auto insurance - Due on the 10th	220.00				220.00						220.00	
License plates - both cars - Due in March							425.00					
Cell phones - Due on the 18th	85.00				85.00				85.00			
Cable TV - Due on the 25th	135.00				135.00				135.00			
Water - Due on the 10th	40.00				40.00						40.00	
Gas - Due on the 28th	95.00				95.00				95.00			
Electricity - Due on the 10th			60.00				60.00				60.00	
Visa - Due on the 15th	110.00				110.00				110.00			
Miscellaneous			75.00	Dentist								
Total paid with checks or EFT	1370.00		1120.00		1370.00		1515.00		1110.00		1305.00	
Items to be paid with Cash:												
Groceries	140.00		140.00		140.00		140.00		140.00		110.00	
Bill's Auto Gas	80.00		80.00		80.00		80.00		80.00		80.00	
Vicki's Auto Gas	50.00		50.00		50.00		50.00		50.00		50.00	
Allowances (Vicki 40, Bill 40)	80.00		80.00		80.00		80.00		80.00		80.00	
Housing Allowance	35.00		35.00		35.00		35.00		35.00		0.00	
Entertainment	60.00		60.00		60.00		60.00		60.00		45.00	
Miscellaneous												
Total paid with cash	445.00		445.00		445.00		445.00		445.00		365.00	
Savings to be set aside												
Savings - Emergency fund	25.00		25.00		25.00		25.00		25.00		25.00	
Savings - Vacation	50.00		50.00		50.00		50.00		50.00		0.00	
Savings - Christmas gifts												
Savings - Retirement	50.00		50.00		50.00		50.00		50.00		50.00	
Other												
Total savings to be set aside	125.00		125.00		125.00		125.00		125.00		75.00	
Money Left Over/Short	(240.00)		10.00		(240.00)		15.00		20.00		(45.00)	

Figure 10

After a brief discussion Bill & Vicki plug in the numbers for the convertible (see above) into their budget. Notice the Money Left Over line. It's **_negative_** once every month.

The budget is saying, "Unless you are willing to make some cuts buying this vehicle doesn't work!"

Seeing those negative numbers Bill says, "Let's plug in the figures for the truck."

When they did that here's how their budget looked….

A Better Solution!

Bill & Vicki's Budget	Pay Date Jan 15th	Notes	Pay Date Jan 31st	Notes	Pay Date Feb 15th	Notes	Pay Date Feb 28th	Notes	Pay Date Mar 15th	Notes	Pay Date Mar 31st	Notes
Checking Account												
Bill's take home pay	850.00		850.00		850.00		850.00		850.00		850.00	
Vicki's take home pay	850.00		850.00		850.00		850.00		850.00		850.00	
Checking account												
Cash												
Other							400.00	Tax Refund				
Total available to pay bills	1700.00		1700.00		1700.00		2100.00		1700.00		1700.00	
Bills to be paid by check or EFT												
Place of worship	135.00		135.00		135.00		180.00		135.00		135.00	
Apartment Rent - Due on the 1st			850.00				850.00				850.00	
Bill's Truck payment	300.00				300.00				300.00			
Auto insurance - Due on the 10th	145.00				145.00						145.00	
License plates - both cars - Due in March							425.00					
Cell phones - Due on the 18th	85.00				85.00				85.00			
Cable TV - Due on the 25th	135.00				135.00				135.00			
Water - Due on the 10th	40.00				40.00						40.00	
Gas - Due on the 28th	95.00				95.00				95.00			
Electricity - Due on the 10th			60.00				60.00				60.00	
Visa - Due on the 15th	110.00				110.00				110.00			
Miscellaneous			75.00	Dentist								
Total paid with checks or EFT	1045.00		1120.00		1045.00		1515.00		860.00		1230.00	
Items to be paid with Cash:												
Groceries	140.00		140.00		140.00		140.00		140.00		110.00	
Bill's Auto Gas	80.00		80.00		80.00		80.00		80.00		80.00	
Vicki's Auto Gas	50.00		50.00		50.00		50.00		50.00		50.00	
Allowances (Vicki 40, Bill 40)	80.00		80.00		80.00		80.00		80.00		80.00	
Housing Allowance	35.00		35.00		35.00		35.00		35.00		0.00	
Entertainment	60.00		60.00		60.00		60.00		60.00		45.00	
Miscellaneous												
Total paid with cash	445.00		445.00		445.00		445.00		445.00		365.00	
Savings to be set aside												
Savings - Emergency fund	25.00		25.00		25.00		25.00		25.00		25.00	
Savings - Vacation	50.00		50.00		50.00		50.00		50.00		0.00	
Savings - Christmas gifts												
Savings - Retirement	50.00		50.00		50.00		50.00		50.00		50.00	
Other												
Total savings to be set aside	125.00		125.00		125.00		125.00		125.00		75.00	
Money Left Over/Short	85.00		10.00		85.00		15.00		270.00		30.00	

Figure 11

Well that's a lot better! The "Money Left Over/Short" line is all positive! There are no shortages! Seeing that the budget will still be in balance they both agree that the truck fits best into their financial plans.

Bill and Vicki both realize that having a convertible would be nice but the monthly payment ($550) is considerably more than the $355 payment they have been paying. That $550 payment along with the $75 increase for auto insurance would exceed the money they have to spend. Unless they were willing to reduce something in their budget (for example vacation savings, allowances, or entertainment budget) they cannot afford it.

In this case having a budget has helped them avoid getting in debt over their head and maybe helped them avoid having arguments about money every month.

When you use your budget in this way the budget facts speak for themselves. It is not his or her opinion. It is your budget facts saying… "This is what you have." And "This is what you can afford."

In this example having a **Basic Budget** keeps Bill & Vicki from unknowingly getting into a situation where their monthly bills exceed what they make.

Having made the wise decision together they decide to celebrate avoiding a serious financial mistake. They agree to use a portion of their entertainment money to buy dinner.

That is good news because now Bill will not have to cook! ☺

Final Thoughts

Well there you have it! The **Basic Budget**!

In a reasonable period of time you **CAN** build a basic budget which will…

1) Help you see where your money is going.
2) Help you identify pay periods when the bills will exceed the cash you have available. This allows you to adjust your bill payment strategy to avoid using credit, spending savings or borrowing money to pay the bills due at that time.
3) Help you make plans to regularly set aside savings for vacations, holiday presents, and major purchases. Do that and you will be able to eliminate paying the interest charges that come when you pay for them with a credit card.
4) Help you evaluate the impact of a large purchase you want to consider.
5) Help you eliminate wasteful spending habits.
6) Help you reduce the stress in your relationship caused by uncontrolled spending habits.
7) Help you achieve your financial goals.

Give **Basic Budgeting** a try. In an evening or two you can put yours together.

Do it and use it and I think your life will be happier! And you will have a lot less stress!

To help you get started a list of common budget items and a blank **Basic Budget** worksheet is included in the back of this booklet.

In addition a list of my top ten cost saving ideas is included on the next page.

Email me and let me know how Basic Budgeting is working for you. I look forward to hearing your stories.

Enjoy the journey!

Bill Byrd
Email: BillVickiByrd@att.net

My Top Ten Ways to Save Money!

A good friend asked me to include this list of tips. I hope they help you save some cash.

1. **Know how to shop for groceries.**

   The grocery is one place most Americans waste hundreds of dollars every year! My wife does a number of things to stretch our food dollars.

   First, she has a budget!

   We get paid every two weeks. She gets a set amount every payday for groceries! She goes to the store knowing what she has to spend, nothing more.

   She has a grocery list!

   She takes a list with her. The list helps eliminate impulse buying. If an item is not on the list she doesn't buy it unless it is something we use and it is on sale at a great price!

   She researches where to go every time!

   My wife looks at the ads in our Sunday paper to see what is on sale. She notes which stores have buy-one-get-one/two–free offers.

   She eats before she goes to the store!

   You've probably done this. Go to the store hungry and everything looks good. Before you know it you've got $30 to $40 worth of stuff in you cart that you didn't plan to buy. There goes the budget and the diet!

   She takes her coupon box!

   My wife has a small plastic box with dividers and a calculator. She uses it to organize the different coupons she saves for grocery shopping. She puts that box in the grocery cart and pulls out the coupons she needs as she shops. On average she saves $8 each time she goes grocery shopping using coupons.

   Take that times 26 paydays and Coupons save us $208 or more each year. That's nearly $300 before tax dollars.

   She goes by herself!

   If I go with her I push the cart. She's checking her coupons and doing unit price checks. I'm looking around throwing stuff in the cart she wouldn't get if I weren't there. To control your food budget let the grocery shopper go to the store alone!

She checks unit prices!

What size laundry detergent should you buy to get the best deal? Often the store wants us to think the giant size is the best deal! Guess what! The large size is not always the best deal! You may not like checking unit cost, but over time doing it will save you a bunch of money!

She shops at a grocery store!

Gas stations sell gas at near cost. They make a lot of their money selling us items we should buy at a grocery store. Convenience stores proclaim to make shopping easy but it costs us a lot more. Besides they don't take coupons! Buy the groceries you need at the grocery and you'll save a lot of money.

She looks for special deals on items we will use!

We will exceed our spending budget for groceries when items we use are on sale at really good prices. Items that we can store are great candidates for this exception: paper products, canned goods, laundry detergent and toiletry items are examples.

Here's my thinking on this. The bank will pay me a few percentage points for money I have deposited. Say $2 a year for $100 of my money. If my wife can take that $100 and buy $150 worth of items we will be using that saves us $50!!! Which is the better way to use $100? I think it's a no brainer!

NOTE – Sometimes you can only get two specially priced items per visit! There's nothing that says you can't go to the store twice that week!

2. **Eating out – Don't overdo it!**

Americans are eating out more and more. Make sure those "eating out" expenses are part of your budget. When you do go out to eat here are some cost saving tips to consider.

- o Meal Share – Today's restaurants serve huge portions. Almost every plate goes back with food left on it! Whenever possible we share one meal! It avoids waste, keeps our waist more trim, **and** saves almost half the cost of the meal.

- o If the restaurant offers free Refills we always buy small drinks! Not Medium or large! **Free refills means you get a large drink for the price of a small!**

- o Better yet, drink water when you eat out. It's free and better for you!

- o Sometimes we even go out, use a two-for-one coupon, get two sandwiches for the price of one, and then take them home to eat where we have our own drinks and chips waiting!

3. Take your lunch!

How often do you eat lunch at work? Every day probably!

We think, "Hey, it's not much to spend $4, $5 maybe $6. What's the big deal!"?
Well let's look at what that lunch REALLY COSTS!

Say you spend $5 for lunch per day, work 5 days a week, and you work 50 weeks a year.
You will spend $1,250 cash per year just for lunch!

<u>Why not take a sack lunch from home and save the money!</u>

4. Do the Math!

Remember those math classes you hated so much in school? This is where they finally pay off!

Here's the kind of stuff we see in ads all the time. You tell me, "Which is better?"

1) Buy one item at full price ($20) and get the second item at half price!

   Or

2) 2) Buy two ($20 each) and get 50% off?

   Those ads sound kind of the same. Well they aren't at all! Two items at sale number one cost $30. (One at $20 plus one for $10) While two items at sale number two only cost $20! ($40/2 = $20) Carry a calculator. It will save you lots of money!

5. Treat Your House Like a Bank!

Put some extra money in it on a regular basis! Add an extra $50 to your monthly house payment and save big bucks!

Example: $100,000 mortgage, 30 years, 6% Interest, Monthly Payment $599.
Interest paid: $115,838 over thirty years.

But, pay an extra $50 each month and you will save $24,500 in interest and pay off your house in less than 25 years!

6. Do it yourself!

This just happened the other day! We wanted to get our car washed at one of those drive through places. They are very convenient. You sit in the comfort of your car while their drive through system cleans your car. It's also pretty expensive. Ours is currently about $7 a wash!

It was a nice day and we drove over to clean up the van using the coupons someone gave us. The line was three cars a breast, bumper to bumper, out to the street and up to the stop sign at the corner!

Amazingly, I looked to one side and there were three "do-it-yourself" bays at the same car wash with no line. I pulled over there and did it myself for $2! We drove off with a clean car while everyone else sat there waiting to spend more money to have their system do the same thing I had just done! And I still had the coupon for the $7 car wash to use later!

7. Go to Garage Sales!

Our part of the country has a lot of garage and yard sales. We've learned over the years that they are a great place to buy things you need at greatly reduced prices.

Everything from furniture to children's clothing and toys is offered often in like new condition. Our "fair price" rule says that an item in good condition should cost about 10% of what it would cost if it were a new item! Anything less is a great deal. If something is in really good condition we'll pay 20% of its new price. Anything above that is suspect.

We've bought lots of toys; playground equipment, clothes, and videos. Our kids found that their allowance went a long way at yard sales. They could buy like new games and toys for a quarter or fifty cents. It was a way to stretch the allowance they earned.

8. Barter!

This is an old idea but it still works! I have a skill you need. You have an item I would like to have. We make a deal. I do some work for you. You give me the item I want. Pretty simple – but it is cheap!

Say the neighborhood handyman needs a baby sitter. Your kitchen sink has a leaky faucet! You watch his children one evening this week. He will fix your sink on Saturday! Neither one of you has to spend a nickel!

9. The Library - Best Deal Around!

Why would you waste money buying or renting all your books, CDs, DVDs, and Videos when the library will loan them to you for *free*?

Do you rent videos? The library in your neighborhood lends them out for free! Plus you can keep them longer! In our case you can get some for three weeks.

Do you like music CDs? The library lends those too! Our library allows us to check out twelve at a time!

No lines either! You can reserve all of these on-line! The library will even send you an email when the items you reserve come in!

10. **Buy Your Straw Hats in the Fall!**

Bernard Baruch, the wealthy financier said when asked the secret of his success, "I buy my straw hats in the fall!"

The point? Buy things when they are sold at the lowest price. Buy sweaters and coats in the spring. Buy lawn care items, straw hats, summer shirts and swimsuits when they are being cleared out, in the fall. You'll get the same new items at greatly reduced prices!

1. Items you may want to include in your budget

Keep in mind that there will be a number of expenses that come up during the year which you do not anticipate when you put your budget together. (Class outings at school, Little League fees, Glasses for the kids, braces etc.) When they occur add them to the Miscellaneous line in your budget. If you expect these to occur again add a new budget line and keep it there so when you start your next budgeting period you will have it in your plan.

Check or EFT

Place of worship donations	Utilities – Gas	Lawn care
Mortgage payments	Utilities – Oil	Snow removal
Extra Mortgage payments	Utilities – Water	Doctor
Rent	Utilities – Sewage	Dentist
Insurance – Auto	Utilities – Cable TV	Prescriptions
Insurance – Life	Utilities – Internet	Nursing care
Insurance – Home	Cell Phone	Newspapers
Insurance – Renters	Auto repair or maintenance	
Utilities – Electricity	Telephone	

Cash

Clothing	Adult Allowances	Haircuts
Groceries	Children's allowances	Housing needs
Auto – Gas	Birthday gifts	
Entertainment	Anniversary gifts	

Savings

Children's education	Retirement	Remodeling project
Vacation	Next car purchase	
Emergency fund	Special purchases	

The next page is a three month worksheet you can use to begin putting your budget together.

Our Budget	Pay Date		Pay Date	Pay Date		Pay Date	Pay Date		Pay Date	
		Notes		Notes		Notes		Notes		Notes		Notes

Money available to pay bills

Total available to pay bills

Bills to be paid by check or EFT

Total paid with checks or EFT

Items to be paid with Cash:

Total paid with cash

Savings to be set aside

Total savings to be set aside

Money Left Over/Short